100

D0601431

DEMCO

Candles, Bubble Baths
& Other Romantic Indulgences

Candles, Bubble Baths & Other Romantic Indulgences

Make Beautiful Gifts to Give (or Keep)

KELLY RENO

PRIMA HOME
An Imprint of Prima Publishing
3000 Lava Ridge Court
Roseville, California 95661
(800) 632-8676 • www.primalifestyles.com

PRIMA PUBLISHING and its colophon are registered trademarks of Prima Communications, Inc. GOOD GIFTS FROM THE HOME is a trademark of Prima Communications, Inc.

DISCLAIMER: THE EXPRESS PURPOSE OF *CANDLES, BUBBLE BATHS & OTHER ROMANTIC INDULGENCES* IS TO PROVIDE SUGGESTIONS FOR A RECREATIONAL HOBBY. THE AUTHOR AND PUBLISHER DISCLAIM ANY WARRANTY OR GUARANTEE, EXPRESS OR IMPLIED, FOR ANY OF THE RECIPES OR FORMULAS CONTAINED HEREIN AND FURTHER DISCLAIM ANY LIABILITY FOR THE READER'S EXPERIMENTS OR PROJECTS. THE AUTHOR OR PUBLISHER DO NOT ASSUME ANY LIABILITY FOR ANY DAMAGES THAT MAY OCCUR AS A RESULT OF READING OR FOLLOWING ANY OF THE RECIPES OR FORMULAS IN THIS BOOK. THE PURCHASE OF THIS BOOK BY THE READER WILL SERVE AS AN ACKNOWLEDGMENT OF THIS DISCLAIMER AND AN AGREEMENT TO HOLD THE AUTHOR AND PUBLISHER HARMLESS FOR ANY MISTAKES THE READER MAY MAKE AS A RESULT OF FOLLOWING THE RECIPES AND FORMULAS IN THIS BOOK.

Library of Congress Cataloging-in-Publication data on file.

00 01 02 03 04 HH 10 9 8 7 6 5 4 3 2 1

Printed in the United States of America

How to Order

Single copies may be ordered from Prima Publishing, 3000 Lava Ridge Court, Roseville, CA 95661; telephone (800) 632-8676, ext 4444. Quantity discounts are also available. On your letterhead, include information concerning the intended use of the books and the number of books you wish to purchase.

Visit us online at www.primalifestyles.com

❧ Especially for my sister, Kyle. May you and Andy always have candlelight that burns as brightly and truly as your love. And to Alicia and Trey: Welcome to our family.

CONTENTS

. . . .

. . . .

ACKNOWLEDGMENTS

. . . .

❧ ABOVE ALL, I would like to thank the readers and followers of my previous books. You have given me so much encouragement and overwhelming support. It is for your use and enjoyment that I've created and written this new book. Many of you have written to me, sharing your successes—they always bring a smile to my face. Some of you have used the recipes to turn this craft into a business for yourselves, which makes me very happy and proud. Thanks again for reading and "sudsing!"

I would also like to thank my father, Michael, and stepmom, Sally, for their support in everything I do. And to Fred, my husband, who unconditionally backs up all my projects and doesn't complain when I cook up new soap recipes instead of dinner.

I would also like to extend special thanks to Darryl Chapman from General Wax and Cari Butler from Earth Potions, both professional candlemakers who helped me perfect the candle recipes in this book. And many thanks to the staff at General Wax who supported this project and provided me with all of my candlemaking supplies and equipment.

. . . .

. . . .

❧ FROTHING, FOAMING bubble baths and soaps, fragrant toiletries, and glowing candles are a few of life's little luxuries. Turning them into simple, homemade gifts is the perfect way to pamper friends, family, and guests—not to mention yourself. Making aromatic, soothing delights—concocted with loving care—in your very own kitchen is a fine way to wrap up and give away a piece of your personal creativity. Send a personal message to recipients that lets them know you care and are thinking of them.

For me, nothing is more relaxing than taking a long, soothing bath by the warm glow of candlelight. All the recipes and instructions you're about to dive into have been prepared with luxury and romance in mind. I hope that this book, in addition to being fun, will inspire your creativity and delight your senses. Enjoy!

. . . .

CHAPTER ONE

Delightful Candles

UNDENIABLY, ONE of life's little pleasures is bathing by candlelight. You can turn just about any ordinary bathroom into a relaxing paradise by adding flickering candles here and there. Small shelves along the walls, windowsills, and countertops are wonderful places to display candles. Or, be a little more creative and use an old lantern or wrought-iron chandelier to add instant romance and rustic charm to your bathroom.

The average person spends at least an hour a day in this little room, so why not make it a special place? Be creative and have fun when you decorate with candles, but be sure you pay attention to safety. Never leave a candle unattended, and keep your candles far away from items that can easily catch fire.

Introduction to Basic Candlemaking

Candles make great gifts for all occasions and nicely complement the décor of any home. Crafting your own candles at home is fun, and so simple that even a beginner can make beautiful candles by following a few basic guidelines. Candlemaking is, in fact, an *ideal* craft for beginners. If you're not satisfied with any of your projects, you can just melt them and start over again. But before you know it, you'll be pouring your own lovely candles—and you may never need to *buy* candles again!

The projects you'll find here are particularly suited for lighting up your bathroom. But before you begin, please pay close attention to everything you read—so you *don't* have to learn the hard way.

Wax

Wax is the basic ingredient of candles. There are different types of wax suitable for different types of candle projects; we'll discuss those types here. Most candles are made from paraffin-based wax, derived from crude oil and processed into different grades that melt at different temperatures.

A paraffin wax that has a melting point of approximately 130° F is soft and ideal for candles that are poured into containers made of glass, ceramic, or other suitable materials. When you use a soft wax for container projects, you'll find that the wax conforms nicely to the container and doesn't leave a ring of unmelted wax around the edges.

When you make pillar or other molded, freestanding candles, you'll need to use a paraffin wax with a higher melting point, 135 to 140° F or greater. This type of wax—hard and sturdy—is particularly suitable for use with metal and other types of molds.

Beeswax is a natural wax made by bees to store their honey. In its natural form, it has a yellowish color and a faint honey scent when burned. Because beeswax has a melting point of approximately 145° F, it makes wonderful molded candles.

Wax Additives

You can create a number of special effects for your candles by adding certain ingredients (called candle additives) to the wax.

As a general guideline when you are making most basic candles, additives (with the exception of coloring and fragrance) are not essential. If you do decide to experiment with an additive, start off by adding no more than 1 teaspoon of it to every pound of melted wax. (If you use stearic acid, you can add 2 to 3 tablespoons per pound.) Once you've combined an additive to your melted wax, stir it well for a few minutes to ensure that it's been blended properly. As you become more experienced at making candles, you may discover that you prefer a little more or a little less of such additives as these:

❧ *Stearic acid,* a candle additive in the form of small, white flakes, is derived from animal fat. Adding it to wax helps harden candles and makes them burn for a longer period of time. You'll usually add 2 to 3 tablespoons of this additive to 1 pound of wax.

❧ *Keramide Mold Release,* a white powder that you can add to wax to make the unmolding process simple and easy. Generally add 1 teaspoon of this additive to 1 pound of wax. Mold release powders work with all types of candle molds.

❧ *Vybar,* a candle additive that helps lock in the color and scent of a candle. It comes in small, white pellets that you can add to the wax. Generally add 1 teaspoon of the additive to 1 pound of wax.

❧ *Polyethylene powder,* or *Poly-Ac,* a fine, white powder. Add 1 teaspoon of this additive to 1 pound of wax to make the finished candle glossy and hard.

The projects in this book cover basic candlemaking projects so will not include additives except for the mold-release powder. As you experiment more with making candles, you can try the various additives to determine which ones work best for you.

Color

If you want to add color to your candles, I recommend you use color chips. Made of wax and dye, these chips can create just about any color. Each manufacturer provides usage guidelines on the package, usually suggesting one chip per pound of wax. If you want to make a pastel candle, mix together color and white chips. To make a candle of a deeper hue, double the amount of color chips. To darken the hue, add some black chips.

An easier way to add color to your candles is to insert a colored crayon or two to the melted wax. Crayons are easy to come by and are much less expensive than specialty dyes.

Add colors to wax just before you pour it into molds or containers. Be sure the wax has melted to the correct temperature, then add the coloring and stir until it's well blended. To test the color, spoon out a bit of the melted wax and drop it into a cup of cold water. The color you see when it cools will be the color of the finished candle.

❧ *As a general rule when coloring candles, start off by adding colors slowly. First, add a small amount of color, then gradually add more until you get the desired hue. You can always add more if the color is too light; if it's too dark, the only way you can lighten it again is to add more wax.*

Fragrance

Perhaps the best part of a candle is the aroma. You can purchase fragrances developed specifically for candlemaking that mix well with wax. Although some candlemakers use essential and perfume oils when making candles, I recommend starting off by using candle scents. If you want to experiment with essential or perfume oils, test them in a small project like a votive candle. Some of these oils will work beautifully; others do not mix well with the wax and will pool and ooze out of the candle.

A friend of mine once made a candle and scented it with orange essential oil. When she presented it as a gift, the recipient couldn't wait to try it. Minutes after the wick was lit, the entire top of the candle was aflame! The oil wasn't compatible with the wax and had oozed to the surface and ignited.

There are many bottled fragrance oils available—and in almost every scent imaginable. As a general rule, professional candlemakers use between ½ to 1 teaspoon of fragrance oil per pound of wax. Start off by adding a small amount to the melted wax; then add a little more if you desire a stronger scent. Be careful not to add too much oil because it will leave spots on the candles.

❋ *Use only oil-based fragrances when making candles. Water- or alcohol-based fragrances will ruin your project.*

Wicks

Candlewicks are made from braided cotton thread. Choosing the right wick is important to ensure that your candle burns properly. A wick that is too large will make the candle smoke and drip. If your wick is too small, the melting wax that pools in the middle will extinguish the flame.

You can usually find a guideline for determining the appropriate wick size printed on the wick package. The wick size depends on the diameter of the finished candle. A small wick is suitable for candles with a diameter of up to 2 inches, a medium wick for diameters between 2 and 3 inches, and large wick for diameters of 3 inches or greater. Special wicks with metal clips and a center wire are available for votive and container candles. The little wire—which helps to keep the wick straight—burns off with the wick as the candle burns down.

Candlewicks should be primed or pre-dipped in a coating of wax to ensure even burning. You can buy wicks that have already been primed, or you can prime them yourself. To prime a wick, melt a small amount of wax and place the wick in it. Saturate the wick for a few minutes, then remove it from the wax and lay it flat on a smooth surface so it dries straight. When the candle is finished, trim the wick to about ¼ inch.

Candle Molds

Most candles are made by forming the wax in molds that are available in craft stores and through candlemaking suppliers. Molds come in many shapes, sizes, and materials such as metal, plastic, and rubber. They are further classified as *rigid* or *flexible*. We will craft the candles in this section using the type of mold that is most appropriate for the project.

Wicking a Candle Mold

Before you pour the wax into the mold, make sure you have inserted the wick properly. Pull about 2 inches of the wick through the hole in the bottom of the mold, using a wicking needle if necessary. Secure the wick with a piece of masking tape that covers the hole. Press the tape down firmly and secure with sealing wax.

❖ *Mold-sealing wax is a solid glue substance that can be purchased from candle suppliers. It is extremely helpful.*

When the sealing wax has dried, pull the top of the wick taut and secure it by wrapping it around a skewer, pencil, or crochet needle placed horizontally on the top of the mold. Once the wick is secure and taut, your mold is ready to be filled.

❖ *Most molds have wick holes in them. Just follow the basic wicking instructions given previously.*

Thermometer

Always use a thermometer when melting wax to avoid overheating. Use a candy thermometer and follow heating instructions on the package of wax for the correct melting temperature.

Method

Start by measuring out how much wax you will need for your candle, then add an extra ½ pound or so. Cut the wax into chunks and place in a double boiler. Clip the candy thermometer onto the pan so the end is submerged in the wax. Stir the wax occasionally. Most additives and colorings are added when the wax reaches 175 to 180° F. Stir additives well and continue to heat wax to about 200° F.

❧ *Never leave hot wax unattended.*

Pour the wax slowly into your wicked mold or container and let it cool undisturbed. When wax cools, it shrinks. Use your extra wax to fill in the mold as needed. When the mold is cool, remove the candle. Turn it upside down (the bottom of the mold will be the candle top) and trim the wick appropriately.

Wax is very hard to clean off pots and pans. Use an old pan reserved just for melting wax, or purchase a tall metal melting container made especially for candlemaking that will fit inside your double boiler.

ASIAN CANDLE

....

❧   *This sweet, mystical candle is perfectly suited for its container—an Asian teacup. Chinese dragon motifs are especially attractive for this project; or you can use a plain metal tin.*

Makes 1 candle

> ½ pound soft paraffin wax (with a melting temperature of 130° F), or
>   enough wax to fill container
> 1 light green color chip
> ½ teaspoon green tea candle fragrance oil (optional)
> Asian teacup or round metal tin
> Wick (use narrow votive size with attached wick clip)

Melt wax in a double boiler to 130° F, or according to instructions on wax package. Add color and fragrance and stir gently. Slowly pour wax into cup or tin, filling it halfway. Insert the wick and fill wax to ¼ inch below rim. Let candle set until completely cool. Fill in any cavities with more melted wax and let cool again. Trim wick to ¼ inch.

....

. . . .

❧   *Make these charming candles in delicious dessert scents, perfect for use when entertaining friends. Light them as you set up the dessert table to fill the air with a scrumptious aroma.*

Makes 3 candles

> 1½ pounds soft paraffin wax (with a melting point of 130° F)
> 3 small ceramic dessert cups
> Color chips—brown for cappuccino and chocolate mint, ivory for crème brulée
> ½ teaspoon fragrance oil—chocolate mint for a chocolate mint candle, coffee for cappuccino, vanilla for crème brulée.
> Three wicks with votive clips attached (clips optional)

Melt soft wax in a double boiler to 130° F. Pour a small amount of wax into one ceramic cup and add appropriate color and fragrance. Fill the cup halfway and insert wick. Fill to just below the rim with wax. Let candles set until completely cool. Fill in any gaps with melted wax. Trim the wicks to ¼ inch. Repeat process for remaining two candles.

. . . .

SNOWFLAKE CANDLE

....

❧   *Add a touch of style to your home with snowflake candles, the latest trend in candlemaking. These unusual candles appear to have tiny snowflakes suspended inside. The trick to making these candles is to add extra oil, which reacts with the wax and creates tiny white spots on the surface.*

Makes 1 candle

> Wick
> Metal candle mold (round or square)
> 1 pound paraffin wax (with a melting temperature of 135 to 140° F)
> Pouring pitcher
> 1 or 2 color chips (your choice)
> Mineral oil (2 tablespoons per pound of wax used)
> 1 teaspoon candle fragrance oil (optional)

Wick the candle mold. Melt wax in a double boiler. Place wax in pouring pitcher and stir in coloring, mineral oil, and fragrance oil. Slowly pour wax to the top of mold. Add more melted wax if needed to fill in cavities. Let the candle set until completely cool. Release from mold and trim wick to ¼ inch. There will be a bit of oil residue on your candle and mold. Wipe it off with an absorbent cloth.

....

BEESWAX TRIO

....

❧ *These lovely beeswax candles are adorned with words from the heart—your heart. As these candles burn, the natural aroma of honey will sweeten the room. Inscribe a favorite quote or poem on this trio of candles and give as a gift to someone special.*

Makes 3 candles

> 3 wicks
> Square candle mold
> Beeswax 1 to 2 pounds
> Stylus (or unfilled calligraphy pen)
> Black tempera paint

Wick your mold for the first candle. Melt wax in a double boiler and stir until liquefied. Remove from heat and pour into prepared mold. Let set until com-

....

pletely cool. Fill in any cavities with more melted wax and let cool. Remove from mold. Repeat melting and pouring for other two candles.

When candles are cool, carve a poem or a message into their sides using a stylus or unfilled calligraphy pen. To do this, carve the words as deeply as possible. Place a small amount of tempera paint on your finger and rub it into the carving. Let it dry for twenty minutes, then rub off surface excess with a tissue. Trim the wick to ¼ inch.

❋ *Use gold leaf instead of tempera paint for a dazzling effect. Break up your poem or message into three parts and write one part on each candle. Then give the set as a special gift.*

SEASHELL CANDLES

....

✳ *Your favorite seashells and the warm ambience of candlelight can be part of your own little paradise. Choose large or small seashells for this delightful, inexpensive project. A dusting of pale pink mica gives these little treasures a pearly glow.*

> Seashells (any size)
> Several flat pebbles, as needed
> Glue gun
> Soft paraffin wax (with a melting temperature of 130° F)
>   to fill your shells
> Pinch of pink, pearly mica dust
> Wicks (use narrow votive type for oyster shells and thicker wicks for larger
>   shells such as abalone)

Clean your shells with warm soapy water and make sure they are dry. If your shells rock or tilt, remedy this by adhering small flat pebble feet to the bottom using a hot glue gun. Arrange pebbles securely so the shell opening is horizontal.

....

Melt wax to 130° F in a double boiler and remove from heat. Stir a pinch of mica dust into the wax and pour a bit of wax mixture into each shell. While the wax is still warm, insert a wick into each candle, making sure that it stands straight in the center of the shell. When set, fill the rest of each shell. Let candles set until completely cool. Trim wicks to ¼ inch.

❈ *The amount of candles you get from this recipe depends completely on the size of your seashells.*

❧ *This candle project comes from a friend, Cari Butler of Earth Potions, who produces a very successful line of bath, body, and candle items. Because her products are so stylish and creative, I asked her to share one of her latest projects with us. You will be delighted by this simple, elegant container candle.*

Makes 1 candle

> 1 pound soft wax (with a melting temperature of about 130° F)
> 1 teaspoon fragrance oil (optional)
> One frosted glass 11-ounce tumbler (3 to 4 inches high)
> Wick with metal clip attached (1 inch taller than your container height)
> Cellophane bag
> Cream-colored ribbon

Melt wax in a double boiler. When liquefied, remove from heat and stir in fragrance oil. Slowly pour wax into tumbler until it reaches ½ inch from the top. Let wax cool a bit and then place prepared wick in the center. If wax is still hot and wick moves away from center, crisscross two chopsticks or pencils over top of container and wrap wick around them securely. Fill in any gaps with melted wax. Let candle cool for twenty-four hours. Then trim the wick to ¼ inch, place candle in a cellophane bag, and tie with ribbon.

....

❋ *To remove scars or blemishes from your candle, put a little bit of turpentine on a cloth and rub it gently over the area until it is smooth.*

Container Candle Ideas

❋ Use container candles for perfect wedding or party favors.

❋ Create fabulous labels for your candles. Paint or print directly on paper labels and adhere to your container.

❋ Add vanilla, peppermint, or lavender fragrance to make your candle even more enticing.

❋ Add a few color chips to the wax. For wrapping, Cari suggests using a contrasting ribbon to complement your candle color.

SURPRISE CANDLE

....

❧ *Not only will this little candle cast a warm, glowing light; but as it melts down,
it will reveal a little silver surprise.*

Makes 1 candle

> Wick
> Metal candle mold (round or square)
> 1 pound wax (with a melting temperature of 135 to 140° F)
> Color chips (your choice)
> 1 teaspoon fragrance oil (optional)
> Small silver or pewter charm or coin (or use several if you like)

Wick the candle mold and set aside. Melt wax in a double boiler to 135° F and
add color and fragrance. Fill ⅓ of the mold and let it set until the wax forms a
skin that should give, but not break, when gently prodded (this takes approximately 10 minutes, depending of the size of the mold). Reheat the remainder of
the wax.

Place the charm or charms on top of the first layer (between the wick and
the sides of the mold), then fill the rest of the mold, covering the charm(s). Fill
in any cavities with melted wax. Let the candle set until completely cool, then
remove from mold. Trim the wick to ¼ inch.

....

✳ *Make sure you place the charm or charms as far away from the wick as possible, but not against the candle sides where they can be seen.*

Wrap this candle in clear cellophane and tie it at the top with pretty ribbon. Be sure to attach a tag that informs the recipient that there is a little treasure inside the candle. You wouldn't want the surprise to accidentally get tossed out with a half-burned candle.

Surprise Candle Ideas

✳ Use bracelet charms or any other small solid metal charms for this project.

✳ Add surprise charms to your candle projects by following these instructions. Just be sure that the surprises are made from metal or other nonflammable material. Crystals work well, too.

✳ Give surprise candles to your bridesmaids.

✳ Try making a "charming chunk candle." Fill the empty mold with chunks of colored wax. Place charms on top of chunks, then fill mold with melted wax.

FLORAL CANDLE

....

❧   *You've probably seen candles like these on the shelves of gift shops and boutiques. They are wide pillar or square candles with dried flowers suspended inside. These dramatic candles are easy to create, and you can use a range of adornments to make your candle unique. Because adding items directly into the wax of the candle would be unsafe (most foreign objects can burn), start with a candle smaller than your mold as the base, then place your dried flowers in the empty space around it before you fill it in with wax.*

   Following are instructions for making a basic candle, accented with pretty decorations.

Makes 1 candle

> 4-inch-wide by 8-inch-tall white pillar candle
> 6-inch-wide by 8-inch-tall metal pillar mold
> Dried or silk flower petals
> ½ cup of small wax chunks (optional)
> 2 pounds white wax (with a melting temperature of 135 to 140° F)
> ½ teaspoon fragrance oil (optional)

Place the pillar candle in the middle of the mold. Arrange dried flower petals in the space between the mold and candle. To prevent them from sinking to the

....

bottom, layer them with the wax chunks. Melt the wax, add fragrance, then gently pour the melted wax into the mold until it covers the pillar candle; leave about ¼ inch of wick sticking up. While wax is still liquefied, gently prod the petals and wax chunks to release any trapped air bubbles. Fill in any cavities with melted wax. Let candle set until completely cool, then remove from mold.

Other Ideas

✿ Use coffee beans, leaves, seashells, or other enhancements instead of flower petals—even hard candies work well!

✿ Experiment using Plexiglas pillar molds for this project. They are ideal because you can view the arrangement before you unmold the candle.

✿ Use an easier way to make a similar candle: Dip dried, pressed flowers or leaves into hot wax and press them onto the outside of a plain pillar candle. Then, brush a layer of hot wax over flowers and let dry.

Warning: *Candles with flammable material on the outside—or on the inside—can be a fire hazard. Burn these candles with particular caution and never leave them (or any candles) unattended.*

SWEET-LIGHT CANDLE

....

❧ *This lovely layered pillar candle smells and looks good enough to eat. Its frosted appearance comes from a coating of pure sugar.*

Makes 1 candle

> Wick suitable for a large candle
> Metal pillar mold (any size)
> 2 pounds paraffin wax (with melting point of 140° F), or enough to fill the
>   mold and have a little extra
> Pouring pitcher
> 2 color chips
> 2 candle fragrance oils of your choice, 1 teaspoon of each (optional)
> ½ cup granulated sugar
> Paint brush
> White glue

Wick the candle mold. Melt wax in a double boiler to 140° F. Pour half the wax into a pouring pitcher and stir in one color and one fragrance. Pour colored, scented wax into mold, filling it halfway. Let it set partially (not cool completely). (At this point, you may place the mold in a saucepan of cold water to speed up the process.)

You can pour the top layer once the bottom layer has developed a skin that will stretch but not break if poked gently (this takes approximately 10 minutes, depending on the size of the mold). While you're waiting for the first layer to develop a skin, heat the remainder of the wax, and add the second color and fragrance. Stir well and pour the second layer on top of the first. Fill mold to ¼ inch below the top.

❊ *If the bottom layer of the candle is allowed to cool and harden, the top layer will not fuse to it properly. If this occurs, you will have to re-melt the first layer and start over.*

Let the candle set until completely cool. Fill in any gaps with melted wax. When cool, release from mold and trim wick to ¼ inch.

(continues)

(continued from page 25)

....

Spread out ½ cup granulated sugar in a shallow pan. Using a paint brush, cover the outside of the candle with an even coat of white glue. Roll the candle in the sugar until lightly coated and let it dry for three hours. Avoid getting sugar on the top of the candle or near the wick—it could flame.

Sweet-Light Candle Ideas

❦ Create a simple sweet-light candle by following the previous directions to coat a store-bought candle in sugar. You will get the same beautiful effect without the work of making your own candle.

❦ Try making a pure white or ivory pillar. It will be simple and elegant.

❦ Make a diagonally layered candle by tilting the mold to the side while the first layer sets. Then pour in the second layer and stand it upright to set. This creates an intriguing effect.

....

CHAPTER TWO

Bubble Baths & Other Formulas for the Tub

BOUNCY BUBBLES, creamy soaps, and aromatic soaks are luxurious additions to a tub of warm water. In this chapter, you will find simple formulas for creating extraordinary gifts for friends, family, and yourself. As you experiment with the recipes, feel free to substitute your own favorite essential oils for those that I suggest.

In this chapter, you'll also find formulas for creating delectable soaps right in your very own kitchen. From vintage washing balls to fresh carrot soap, this creative collection of recipes provides the secrets of specialty soapmaking. Have fun making these unusual soaps for yourself or as gifts.

These recipes are all about crafting beautiful and beautifying potions, and no one knows more about what is personally beautiful to you, than you. Happy sudsing!

❋ When making bath and body formulas, use only perfume, fragrance, or essential oils intended for adding scent to bath products and cosmetics. Never use potpourri or candle fragrances in these recipes, as they could cause allergic reactions.

Essential Oil or Fragrance Oil?

Before we get started, I'd like to explain to you the difference between the two most popular kinds of oils used—essential oil and fragrance oil. *Essential oil* is the fragrant oil found naturally in flowers, herbs, spices, and leaves. The oil is extracted directly from the plant source, thus capturing the essence. *Perfume or fragrance oils* are man-made fragrances that are either fully synthetic or a combination of synthetic and natural oils that imitate scents found in nature such as pear, peach, or chocolate. Although these particular scents do exist, we have no way to extract their essences from their sources. There are also synthetic copies of essential oils, such as rose or lavender. Because I prefer natural oils over synthetic oils that contain chemicals, I've recommended using essential oils in most of the following recipes. This way, you can add natural fragrance to your soaps and toiletries.

For the Bath

Here you'll find a collection of recipes and formulas to turn your next bath into an extraordinary little escape. Pamper yourself with a tub of fragrant bubbles or silky bath oils, or sink into an aromatic tub tea. Relax and wash away your worries with delightful soaps, toning salts, and other bathing luxuries. Enjoy your bath time—you've earned it!

JASMINE FOAM BATH

✿ The exotic aroma of jasmine makes this foam bath a gem. With extra moisturizing power from pure aloe vera gel, this emerald-colored bubble bath will turn your next bath into a steamy tub of bliss!

⅓ cup foaming concentrate (or ⅔ cup unscented shampoo)
⅓ cup aloe vera gel
⅓ cup sparkling mineral water
10 drops jasmine essential oil
1 tablespoon glycerin
2 drops yellow food coloring
1 drop green food coloring

Combine foaming concentrate and aloe vera gel in a bowl and stir gently until well blended. Gradually add sparkling water into the mixture while stirring. Add essential oil, glycerin, and food coloring, then stir until smooth. Store in a closed bottle, and when ready for a special bath, pour 2 tablespoons under running bath water.

BEE'S BEST HONEY BATH

....

❧ *Step into a tub of silky, blissful bubbles from this honey bath and you'll understand why bees guard their hives so fiercely! Naturally cleansing honey combined with a touch of moisturizing jojoba oil is soothing to the skin and delightful to the senses.*

> 2 tablespoons foaming concentrate (or ¼ cup unscented bubble bath
>   or mild liquid soap)
> 2 teaspoons honey
> ¼ cup purified water
> ¼ cup orange-flower water
> 1 teaspoon jojoba oil
> ½ teaspoon salt
> 2 drops cinnamon essential oil

Combine foaming concentrate, honey, purified water, and orange-flower water in a bowl and stir until well blended. Add jojoba oil, salt, and essential oil, stirring until smooth. Then transfer the honey bath to a bottle. To use, pour 2 tablespoons under running bath water.

❧ *Replace the cinnamon essential oil with sandalwood essential oil for an even more woodsy scent.*

....

LAVENDER BATH OIL

❧ This fragrant, lovely bath oil looks beautiful and works even better. Pure glycerin makes this oil water-soluble, so it will mix with your bath and not float on top. Give a bottle of this deep-purple concoction to a friend or enjoy it yourself.

½ cup glycerin
¼ teaspoon lavender essential oil
3 drops lavender food coloring

Combine glycerin and essential oil in a bowl and stir until well blended. Add food coloring and stir until color is evenly distributed throughout mixture. Then transfer the bath oil to a closed bottle. To use, pour 2 tablespoons under running bath water. Replace the suggested essential oil and coloring with your favorites if desired.

OCEAN MINERAL BATH SOAK

....

❧ *Drench your skin with this mineral-rich bath soak. A combination of salt, borax, and mica dust makes this fragrant formula a beautiful, sparkling addition to any tub.*

> ½ cup sea salt (or table salt)
> 2 tablespoons borax powder
> ¼ teaspoon blue mica dust
> 3 drops sandalwood essential oil

Combine salt and borax in a bowl and stir until blended. Add mica dust and essential oil; mix until color is evenly distributed. Store in a glass jar.

❧ *Use a clean, dry oyster shell as a scoop; place it inside the jar or tie it to the jar with a ribbon.*

. . . .

❧ *Take a dip in a tub filled with bouncy bubbles in fruity sorbet scents. Extra oil is added to this formula for skin nourishment.*

> ¼ cup foaming concentrate (or ¼ cup unscented bubble bath)
> ¾ cup purified water
> ¼ teaspoon salt
> 2 teaspoons mineral oil
> 20 drops raspberry fragrance oil
> 2 drops red food coloring

Combine foaming concentrate and warm purified water in a glass measuring cup and stir gently until well blended. Add salt, mineral oil, fragrance oil, and color, and stir together. Store in a bottle. To use, pour 1 to 2 tablespoons under running bath water.

❧ *You can make other great flavors of sorbet foam. Try mango, orange, or lemon, and use the appropriate food coloring for each. Or make all four flavors and give a set to a friend as a special gift.*

. . . .

BATH FIZZ

....

❧ *Tiny effervescent bubbles add fizz and fragrance to your bath water. This combination of cleansing baking soda, toning cornstarch, and rich vitamin C is a treat for your skin. Use it and let the little bubbles lift your spirits.*

½ cup baking soda
⅛ cup cornstarch
20 drops essential oil (your choice)
⅛ cup citric acid (or crush vitamin C tablets into powder)

Combine baking soda and cornstarch in a bowl and stir until well blended. Gently stir in essential oil, one drop at a time, until well mixed. Then add citric acid and stir gently. Store in a glass jar with a lid in a cool, dry place. To use, add 2 tablespoons to bath for fizzing, fragrant fun.

❧ *Keep your bath fizz formula free from moisture so it will not fizzle out prematurely.*

....

BUTTERMILK BATH SOAK

....

❦   *This so-good-for-your-skin formula is made with real moisturizing buttermilk and will turn your tub into a relaxing spa.*

> 1 cup dry, powdered buttermilk (or powdered milk)
> ¾ cup table salt
> ½ cup baking soda

Combine ingredients in a bowl and stir until well blended. Store in an airtight container. To use, add ½ cup to warm bath water.

❦   *For a thoughtful gift, sew four 2-inch by 4-inch bags from white cotton. Dissolve a few drops of vanilla fragrance oil in a teaspoon of grain alcohol and sprinkle over the mixture. Then fill bags with individual portions of the mixture. For a refreshing soak, float one bag in a warm bath. Discard after use.*

....

TANGERINE TUB TINT

. . . .

❄ *Add a splash of happiness and vibrant color to your next bath with a bottle of bath tint. Although orange is a personal favorite of mine, you may use your favorite colors and fragrances to suit your mood (or match the colors in your bathroom). Try green, pink, yellow, blue, or whatever you fancy!*

> ¾ cup purified water
> ¼ cup aloe vera gel
> 1 tablespoon glycerin
> 1 teaspoon orange liquid food coloring
> ½ teaspoon tangerine essential oil (optional)

Combine all ingredients in a bottle and shake until well blended. Add 1 to 2 tablespoons to bath water. This formula will not stain the tub or skin.

❄ *Make a lemon tub tint by replacing the tangerine essential oil and orange coloring with lemon essential oil and yellow coloring.*

. . . .

37

TUB TEA

. . . .

❧   *There's nothing quite like relaxing in a tub of fragrant bath tea. Tub tea is a special blend of flowers, water-softening agents, and fragrant oils. A set of teas makes an easy and inexpensive gift for any occasion.*

    ¼ cup ground oats
    ¼ cup dried lavender blossoms
    ¼ cup dried rose petals
    1 teaspoon borax powder
    10 drops lavender essential oil
    10 drops rose essential oil
    10 drops tangerine essential oil
    Three 6-inch by 6-inch muslin squares or rounds
    Ribbon

Place oats in a food processor or coffee grinder and chop until they are a fine powder. Set aside. Place lavender blossoms and rose petals in a bowl and bruise them to help release fragrant oils. Stir in ground oats and borax powder until blended. Sprinkle lavender, rose, and tangerine oils over mixture and stir. Divide into thirds, and place each portion in the center of a muslin piece. Gather muslin at the top and secure with a ribbon. To use, drop a bag in warm bath water and swish it around. Discard after use.

❧ *For an unusual gift, place a tub tea bag in a teacup and wrap in a clear, cellophane bag. Tie a purple or red ribbon around the top, and add a tag with instructions.*

CREAMERY BATH BAGS

. . . .

❊ *Throughout the ages, beautiful skin has been attributed to soaking in milk baths. These creamery bath bags will add frothy bubbles and nourishing milk to your bath water.*

Makes 4 bags

> ½ cup powdered milk
> 2 teaspoons foaming concentrate (or 1 tablespoon bubble bath)
> 15 drops jojoba oil
> Pinking shears (optional)
> Four 4-inch squares of fabric
> 4 yards of thin, satin ribbon

Place powdered milk in a bowl and add foaming concentrate and jojoba oil. Stir with a fork until well blended and no lumps remain. Let it sit, uncovered, for a few hours, then re-stir. Using pinking shears (or scissors), cut four 4-inch by 4-inch squares of fabric. Spoon 2 tablespoons of mixture into the center of each fabric square. Gather the corners of the fabric together and secure with a yard of ribbon. Then knot together the ends of the ribbon and store in a cool, dry place. To use, hang the bag by its ribbon loop over the faucet while running your bath water. Discard after use.

❀ *You can also wrap the milk bath like a little gift package. Follow previous directions, but instead of gathering together the corners of the fabric, fold each side of the fabric—like gift wrap—over the milk bath mix and secure with a ribbon. Float the bag directly in your bath water.*

MISS VENABLE'S OATMEAL SOAP

....

❧ *I fell in love with oatmeal soap when I was in the third grade. My teacher, Miss Venable, always kept a bar of this special soap on the sink in our classroom, and we eagerly lined up to wash our hands with it.*

    2 tablespoons ground oats
    1 bar unscented white soap
    ⅓ cup whole milk
    ½ teaspoon sweet almond oil

Grind whole oats to a coarse powder in a food processor or coffee grinder and set aside. Grate the bar of white soap finely with a food processor or cheese grater. In a double boiler, combine grated soap and milk, stirring until the soap has melted. (Be patient, this step may take up to twenty minutes.) When smooth, remove from heat and stir in ground oats and almond oil. Pour mixture into soap mold and let it set for six hours. Remove from mold and let soap air dry for an additional forty-eight hours.

....

CINNAMON BEESWAX SOAP

* *

❧ *This long-lasting soap is ideal for even the most sensitive skin. Made with real honey, moisturizing jojoba oil, and a hint of cinnamon fragrance, this is sure to become a favorite around your household. Its deep, ruby-red color will dress up any bathroom.*

> 4-ounce bar unscented glycerin soap
> ½ teaspoon beeswax, grated
> 2 teaspoons honey
> 1 teaspoon jojoba oil
> 3 drops cinnamon essential oil
> 3 drops red food coloring
> Soap mold
> Cellophane

Melt soap and beeswax in a small saucepan over low heat. Stir gently until liquefied. Remove from heat and add honey, jojoba oil, essential oil, and coloring, stirring until well blended. Pour soap into mold and let set for three hours. Remove from mold and wrap in clear cellophane until ready to use.

* *

CARROT GARDEN SOAP

....

❧ *This fresh, cleansing soap is perfect for washing up after gardening. Real carrot slivers help to gently remove dirt from hands, and jojoba oil and skim milk pamper dry, irritated skin. Scented with a combination of herbal and clover aromas, this soap is anything but garden variety!*

    ½ medium carrot
    1 bar unscented white soap, shredded
    ¼ cup fresh skim milk
    2 teaspoons jojoba oil
    5 drops rosemary essential oil
    5 drops basil essential oil

Finely grate carrot with a cheese grater and set aside. Shred soap with cheese grater or food processor. Place soap, milk, and jojoba oil in a double boiler and stir gently until smooth. This may take a while, so be patient! If soap starts to look dry while melting, add a tablespoon of water.

....

When soap is smooth, remove from heat and stir in carrots and essential oils. Pour into mold and let harden for forty-eight hours. Remove from mold and soap is ready to use.

❋ *Wrap this soap in an empty carrot-seed envelope and tie with an orange ribbon for a charming, country look.*

VINTAGE WASHING BALL

. . . .

✽ *In the old days, balls of soap were often referred to as washing balls. Washing balls similar to this one were widely used during the eighteenth century. The heavenly scent and dried botanicals of this washing ball pleasantly update a classic.*

    2 bars white soap
    1 tablespoon dried rose petals
    1 tablespoon dried lavender flowers
    ½ teaspoon coriander seed
    ½ cup purified water
    10 drops lavender essential oil
    1 drop clove essential oil
    1 drop sandalwood essential oil
    1 tablespoon orrisroot powder

Shred white soap finely with a cheese grater or food processor and set aside. Combine dried rose petals, lavender flowers, and coriander seed in a food processor and chop into fine particles. You can also use a mortar and pestle to crush the mixture. Place shredded soap and water in a double boiler and stir until smooth. Remove from heat and add in essential oils, the chopped flower and coriander mixture, and orrisroot powder. Stir until well blended.

When mixture is cool enough to handle, roll it into one or two balls, using the palms of your hands. Let soap air-dry for seventy-two hours; then it will be ready to use.

CHOCOLATE RASPBERRY BONBON SOAPS

. . . .

❧ *Jazz up your guest bathroom or present a special friend with a box of chocolate-raspberry bonbons—without giving them one single calorie! Sound too good to be true? These tempting confection lookalikes are anything but edible. Although they do look good enough to eat, don't be tempted to taste them. After I put my first batch on the kitchen counter, everyone who passed by asked if they could try one. "Of course," I told them, "but they are soap." These fabulous soaps fooled even the chocoholics in my home.*

Makes 18 miniature soaps

> One 3-ounce unscented white bar soap, shredded
> ¼ cup water
> 20 drops raspberry fragrance oil (optional)
> 5 drops red food coloring
> 1 bar unscented glycerin soap
> 2 tablespoons (about 10 pieces) dark dipping chocolate
> 20 drops chocolate fragrance oil (optional)

❧ *Dipping chocolate is chocolate with extra cocoa butter added to make it melt at a low temperature. It's available in cooking stores or from craft or candy making shops.*

. . . .

Bonbon Filling

Shred the white soap with a cheese grater or food processor set to fine. Combine water and soap in a double boiler, stirring and mashing until the soap melts and forms a sticky mass. Remove from heat and stir in fragrance oil and coloring until smooth. When soap is cool enough to handle, form it into teaspoon-sized balls and set them on a sheet of waxed paper. Let soap balls air-dry overnight.

Bonbon Chocolate Coating

Melt glycerin soap and dipping chocolate in a small saucepan over low heat, stirring gently until mixture is liquefied and well blended. Remove from heat and stir in chocolate fragrance oil. Drop each soap ball into the chocolate soap mixture and turn with a spoon until coated, then place on a nonstick surface. Drizzle the remainder of the chocolate soap over each ball for a thicker coating. Let bonbon soaps set for three hours before using them.

❋ Package your truffle soaps in miniature paper or foil candy cups then arrange the wrapped soaps in a small box. Or place each soap in a candy cup and wrap with cellophane and ribbon. Be sure to let your recipients know that these deliciously scented treats are soap.

FRUITY SOAPSICLES

....

❋ *Pure glycerin soap in gem-like colors is scented with favorite popsicle flavors and shaped in real popsicle molds. A set of these fragrant pops is a happy addition to the side of any tub. Kids love these!*

    1 pound unscented glycerin soap
    ½ teaspoon essential oil (lemon, lime, or orange)
    5 drops food coloring (yellow, green, or orange)
    Six-unit plastic popsicle mold
    Six popsicle sticks
    Cellophane

Place soap in a double boiler and stir gently until liquefied. Immediately remove from heat and stir in essential oil and food coloring. Pour soap into molds and insert popsicle sticks. Let set for three hours. Remove from molds and wrap in clear cellophane.

LUSCIOUS LAVENDER SOAP LOAF

....

❧   *This amethyst loaf of luxury soap—made with the timeless fragrance of lavender and packaged with real lavender flowers—is a beautiful addition to any bathroom. Your friends will be eager to try it.*

> ½ cup dried lavender flowers
> 1 quart milk carton (perfect for 1 pound of soap)
> 1 pound unscented glycerin soap
> ¼ teaspoon lavender essential oil
> 5 drops violet food coloring (available from cake-decorating suppliers)
> Soap mold

Spread dried lavender flowers in the bottom of milk carton mold and set aside. Place soap in a saucepan over medium heat and stir until liquefied. Immediately remove from heat and add lavender oil and coloring, stirring gently until well blended. Pour soap into mold and let set for six hours. Remove from mold and slice into bars as needed.

❧   *The lavender soap loaf makes a perfect hostess gift. Wrap the entire soap brick in a cellophane bag and sprinkle another ¼ cup of lavender flowers into the bag. Enclose a pretty table knife for cutting the soap, and seal the bag with a purple ribbon.*

....

CHAPTER THREE

Other Indulgences for the Body

IN THIS chapter, you'll find many recipes for creating luxurious toiletries to pamper yourself and friends. You'll be delighted and amazed by the simplicity of these fabulous formulas—from silky dusting powders to glittering body lotions.

POWDERED PETAL DUST

. . . .

❧   *Pat on this naturally sweet, silky powder after a relaxing bath for instant fresh-*
ness. Natural rose petals give this powder its subtle sweetness reminiscent of a new-
born baby. This delicate powder needs no additional fragrance oil. For soft, lovely
color try pink petals. Petal dust is a favorite in our household and will be in yours,
too, after you share it with friends, family, and, of course, the wee folk. This powder
makes a perfect baby-shower gift.

    ¼ cup dried rose petals
    ¼ cup cornstarch
    ¼ cup French green clay (or substitute kaolin clay)

Using a coffee grinder or food processor, crush rose petals into as fine a powder
as possible. Then, combine petal dust, cornstarch, and clay in a bowl and stir

gently until well blended. For a stunning effect, drop in a few whole dried petals into the mix. Then, put in a powder box or closed container and store in a cool, dry place.

❋ *For an attractive gift, pour powder into a large salt or cheese shaker and, for perfect dispensing, place a 6-inch circle of pink bridal illusion (veil netting, available at fabric stores) beneath the lid before screwing it on. Fold bridal illusion down over the mouth of the bottle, screw on the lid, and tie a sheer ribbon around the middle of the bottle.*

HONEY GLOW DUSTING POWDER

....

❧ *The next time you feel like stepping out—or staying in—for a romantic evening, try this sheer, shimmering dusting powder. Your skin will be petal soft and glowing with gold radiance. Soothing cornstarch combined with golden mica dust, an all-natural cosmetic coloring, makes this translucent powder a special treat for the body.*

    ⅓ cup cornstarch
    ¼ cup kaolin clay
    2 teaspoons arrowroot powder
    1 teaspoon gold mica dust
    Gold ribbon

Combine all ingredients in a small bowl and stir gently until well blended. Store in a tightly closed box or jar to protect from moisture. Tie a sheer, golden ribbon around your container to add a touch of glamour to this exotic powder.

    ❧ *Store this powder in an antique salt shaker.*

....

SUGARY SPICE BATH POWDER

··

❧ *This velvety bath powder laced with sugar and spice (and everything nice!) is the perfect ending to a relaxing, steamy bath. Pat it on with a thick, fluffy powder puff.*

    ¾ cup cornstarch
    1 tablespoon arrowroot powder
    ¼ teaspoon powdered sugar
    2 drops cinnamon essential oil

Combine cornstarch, arrowroot powder, and powdered sugar in a bowl and stir gently until well blended. Add essential oil, a drop at a time, and stir with a fork until no lumps remain. Keep in a cool, dry place.

❧ *Store this powder in a small, round box and tie with a red ribbon. Affix a few slices of dried apple and a cinnamon stick to the top for a fancy, aromatic gift.*

··

FRENCH VANILLA BUTTER BAR

....

❧ *Drench your skin with a bar of this solid body moisturizer. This moisturizer in bar form is easy to apply and great to use on dry skin. The silky combination of oils soothes your skin as you rub it on after a relaxing bath.*

    2 tablespoons grated beeswax
    2 tablespoons sweet almond oil
    1 tablespoon cocoa butter
    ½ teaspoon jojoba oil
    Candle mold
    Cellophane

Combine beeswax, sweet almond oil, and cocoa butter in a double boiler and stir gently until wax is liquefied. Remove from heat and stir in jojoba oil until well blended. Pour mixture into a 3-ounce soap or candle mold, and let set for two hours. Remove from mold and wrap in cellophane. Store in a cool place.

❧ *Try making the bar with sweet almond oil instead of jojoba.*

....

MINTY RAZZLE DAZZLE GEL

. . . .

❧ *Smooth this glitzy, mint scented gel onto the skin for instant sparkle and shine. It's made with gentle aloe vera gel, glycerin, and lots of pure, natural sparkles.*

⅛ cup aloe vera gel
1 teaspoon glycerin
1 teaspoon purified water
3 drops peppermint essential oil
¼ teaspoon pale green mica dust

Combine aloe vera gel, glycerin, purified water, and essential oil in a small bowl and stir. Add mica dust and stir for a few minutes until well blended. (Mixture will resemble liquid metal.)

❧ *You can always use your own favorite essential oil instead of the mint.*

. . . .

HEAVY CREAM

....

❧   *This ultra-rich cream, a real luxury, is great for restoring moisture to dry skin. Homemade creams are very thick, and a little goes a long way. However, making creams in your home can be a bit tricky, so you will need to follow the recipe and instructions exactly to achieve perfect results.*

> ½ cup white petroleum jelly
> 1 tablespoon grated beeswax
> ¼ cup distilled water
> ½ teaspoon borax powder
> 5 drops essential oil (optional)
> 1 drop food coloring (optional)

Place the petroleum jelly and beeswax in a double boiler and stir occasionally until wax has melted. In a separate small pot, combine distilled water and borax powder and let mixture come to a simmer. When petroleum jelly and beeswax have liquefied, remove from heat. Slowly pour the simmering water and borax into the jelly and beeswax mixture, while briskly stirring with a wire whisk; mixture will turn white and thick. Continue whisking until cream cools to room

....

temperature. Add essential oil and food coloring, if desired, and stir until well blended. Store it in a jar or other closed container. If you like, make a fragrance-coordinated cream and bubble-bath set for a great gift.

Tips for Success

🌿 Avoid a long cleanup by making a disposable double boiler. Put a deep, disposable pie tin over a pot of boiling water. When liquefied, remove tin using pot holders. Keep the petroleum jelly and beeswax mixture in the tin when you add the water and borax mixture, stirring often. Then throw away the tin after you've bottled your cream, and you'll have no greasy pot scrubbing to do.

🌿 Make sure mixtures are very hot when poured together.

🌿 Drizzle in the distilled water and borax a little at a time.

🌿 Stir mixture constantly until completely cool. This may take up to fifteen minutes.

🌿 Add essential oil to this cream and make a fragrance-coordinated bubble bath for a great gift set. This cream does not need to be refrigerated. It will not spoil and, if kept in a closed jar, will last for years.

LIME SPARKLE CREAM

....

❧ *This whimsical cream replaces boring, old lotions. Sparkling mica dust magically lights up the skin; and the sweet, tart lime fragrance smells good enough to eat! Make a batch of this special cream for your best friend.*

½ cup unscented white body lotion
½ teaspoon mica dust (any color)
15 drops lime essential oil

Place lotion in a small bowl and add mica dust, stirring until well blended. Add essential oil and stir. Store in a closed bottle.

VINTAGE MOISTURIZING TONIC

. . . .

❧ *This ancient beauty potion has stood the test of time—for good reason. Invented hundreds of years ago, this formula is possibly the best skin moisturizer known to man. Rosewater gives this tonic a naturally sweet fragrance, and glycerin adds light moisturizing properties. For petal-soft skin, try this simple formula and see for yourself.*

> ½ cup rose water
> ¼ cup distilled water
> ¼ cup glycerin

Combine rose water, distilled water, and glycerin in a bowl and stir until well blended. Store in a bottle.

Special Touches

- ❧ Add a drop of pink food coloring for delicate color.
- ❧ Use an antique bottle to store this vintage formula.
- ❧ Keep this in a bottle with a mister pump, and spritz it on after a bath.

. . . .

....

❧ *This hand gel—made with pure aloe vera gel and germ-fighting alcohol—is a pleasant way to freshen up the hands when water isn't available. Just rub a little between the palms of your hands for instant cleaning.*

½ cup aloe vera gel
¼ cup Everclear grain alcohol (or substitute vodka)
5 drops jasmine essential oil
5 drops tangerine essential oil
3 drops red food coloring

Combine aloe vera gel and alcohol in a bowl and stir until well blended. Add essential oils and coloring, and stir until well mixed. Store in a bottle.

Special Touches

❧ Store in a plastic bottle with a pump or squeeze top for easy dispensing.
❧ Replace the suggested essential oils with your own favorite.
❧ Fill a miniature bottle with this formula and keep it in your purse or pocket. It comes in handy after your toddler has visited the park or petting zoo!

....

BODY GLITTER GEL

....

❦ *Indulge yourself with thousands of glistening sparkles when you smooth on this skin-friendly body gel. Pure aloe vera gel and plenty of glorious glitter make this formula a dazzling treat.*

   ½ cup aloe vera gel
   1 teaspoon jojoba oil
   ¼ teaspoon fine polyester glitter (available in craft stores)
   ¼ teaspoon glycerin
   1 drop food coloring (optional)

Combine aloe vera gel, jojoba oil, glitter, and glycerin in a small bowl. For a special touch, add one drop of food coloring to tint the formula. Stir until well blended. Store in a bottle. Be careful not to get any of this in your eyes.

   ❧ *Do not substitute metal glitter for the polyester glitter, as colors of the metal glitter will run.*

....

. . . .

❧ *Make a batch of this delicious lip balm that helps nourish and protect the lips. A hint of tart cherry is added for lip-smacking flavor.*

    1½ teaspoons cocoa butter
    1½ teaspoons beeswax, grated
    5 drops cherry candy flavoring oil (available from cake-decorating suppliers)

Combine cocoa butter and beeswax in a double boiler and stir gently until liquefied. Remove from heat and stir in candy flavoring oil. Pour into a small screw-top container or tin.

Special Touches

    ❧ Add a bit of color by dropping a ¼-inch piece of dark lipstick into the liquefied wax and cocoa-butter mixture. As the lipstick melts, stir well. For a hint of sparkle, drop in a pinch of mica dust when formula is liquefied. Stir until well blended.

    ❧ Use any variety of a candy-flavored oil you like, or replace with an equal amount of lemon, orange, peppermint, or cinnamon essential oil. (Do not use perfume oils in lip balm.)

. . . .

LEMON-LIME FRAGRANCE NECTAR

....

❧ *Smooth on this gel perfume after a bath for a fresh, fruity fragrance that lasts all day. Aloe vera gel helps to moisturize the skin, too.*

> 2 tablespoons aloe vera gel
> 1 tablespoon Everclear grain alcohol
> 10 drops lemon essential oil
> 10 drops lime essential oil
> 5 drops jojoba oil

Combine aloe vera gel and alcohol in a small bowl and stir until well blended. Stir in essential oil and jojoba oil. Store in a small, closed container or bottle.

❧ *Replace suggested essential oils with ¼ teaspoon of your favorite essential oil.*

....

LAVENDER BATH SPLASH

Bath splashes are used to tone and scent the skin. This violet-tinted formula is bursting with the sweet aroma of lavender. Splash on this bottled bouquet after your next bath.

½ cup 100-proof vodka
¼ cup distilled water
2 tablespoons aloe vera gel
¼ teaspoon lavender essential oil
4 drops violet food coloring

Combine all ingredients in a bottle and shake until well blended. Also shake bottle before each use. Splash onto skin after bathing.

The Gentlemen's Corner

IN THIS special chapter, you'll find recipes for luxurious bath formulas just for men. Homemade aftershaves, shower gels, and other little luxuries are a nice way to pamper the men in your life. Use the suggested essential oils to scent your creations or replace them with masculine essential oils. A few favorites are musk, patchouli, sandalwood, vanilla, cedarwood, amber, pine, and frankincense.

❧ *These gleaming bath crystals—made with the deep, woodsy scent of sandalwood—are a great gift for your favorite man.*

⅔ cup rock salt
30 drops sandalwood essential oil
20 drops yellow food coloring
5 drops red food coloring

Pour rock salt in a bowl. Add essential oil then coloring on top of the fragrance oil. Stir for several minutes with a fork until coloring is evenly distributed. Or, shake the salt, oil, and coloring together in a bottle. Let crystals air-dry overnight and remix them the next day. Keep in a cool, dry place. A glass canister makes a good storage container. To use, add 1 tablespoon to bath water. Bath crystals help to tone the skin and perfume the water. Add a tag with instructions if you are giving as a gift.

CITRUS AFTERSHAVE GEL

··

❧   *This formula is perfect for soothing facial skin after shaving. It is created with aloe vera gel, toning floral water, and alcohol. Tangerine fragrance is added to give it a fresh kick of citrus.*

> ¼ cup aloe vera gel
> ⅛ cup orange-flower water
> ⅛ cup vodka
> 15 drops tangerine essential oil
> 1 drop orange food coloring

Combine all ingredients in a 4-ounce bottle and shake until well blended.

··

....

❦ *The clean freshness of a waterfall is captured in this bottle of aqua-tinted body wash. The invigorating scent and sudsy bubbles will cleanse the body and please the senses.*

⅓ cup purified water
¼ cup foaming concentrate (or ½ cup unscented shampoo)
2 tablespoons aloe vera gel
¼ teaspoon salt
3 drops patchouli essential oil
2 drops aqua food coloring

Place water in a bowl and add foaming concentrate and aloe vera gel, then stir gently until mixture is smooth. Add salt and stir until mixture thickens a bit. Add essential oil and food coloring, then stir gently until well blended. Store in a closed bottle. For variety, try using musk, lime, or sandalwood scents in place of the patchouli fragrance.

❦ *For an inviting gift, use a length of twine to tie a thick white washcloth to the bottle of gel.*

....

TRAVEL COLOGNE

....

❧ *Solid cologne is a great way to carry fragrance when traveling. Make this special blend for your favorite guy to keep his heart close to home—no matter where he is.*

    1 tablespoon white petroleum jelly
    ½ teaspoon beeswax
    ¼ teaspoon essential oil (your choice)

Combine petroleum jelly and beeswax in a double boiler and stir until liquefied. Add in essential oil and stir until well blended. Pour mixture into a small screw-top jar or tin, and let cool for two hours. Make a solid perfume for yourself using the same recipe with your favorite fragrance oils.

❧ *There are about twenty-five drops of essential oil per teaspoon. Make a special combination for your man by custom-mixing his favorite fragrances.*

....

SANDALWOOD SHAVING SOAP

. . . .

❧ *This pure and gentle soap is ideal for men when sudsing up for shaving. Extra oil is added for delicate skin, and the clean scent of sandalwood is always a favorite with men.*

    1 bar unscented glycerin soap
    1 tablespoon mineral oil
    10 drops sandalwood essential oil
    Coffee mug, old shaving mug, or small ceramic bowl
    Shaving brush
    Cellophane bag
    Ribbon

Place soap in a small pan over low heat and stir gently until liquefied. Immediately remove from heat and add mineral oil and essential oil. Stir until blended. Slowly pour soap mixture into mug or bowl and let set for three hours. Place shaving brush on top of mug and wrap in a clear cellophane bag tied with a ribbon. When the soap is gone, refill container with a fresh batch.

. . . .

OLD-TIME BRILLIANTINE

. . . .

❧ *Brilliantine is an old-fashioned hair dressing that men used for styling and shine. The essential oils in this recipe are the same as those in the original formula and will create a vintage brilliantine. To use, rub a scant amount between fingers and apply to hair.*

> ¼ cup castor oil
> 1 tablespoon beeswax, grated
> 10 drops tuberose essential oil
> 5 drops bergamot essential oil
> 5 drops cinnamon essential oil

Combine castor oil and beeswax in a double boiler and stir gently until liquefied. Remove from heat and stir in essential oils until blended. Pour into a wide-mouthed jar or container and allow to completely cool.

. . . .

CHAPTER FIVE

Decorating Ideas for the Bath & Bedroom

THERE ARE many ways to turn ordinary bathrooms and bedrooms into romantic little hideaways. Every room varies in size and potential, offering a range of possibilities. Here are a few effective ideas to help you create rooms that are a pleasure to visit.

For Your Bath

There are many simple ways to add warmth and romance to your bathroom. A great way to add soft light, for example, is by using candles. If you have limited counter space, consider putting up some small wall shelves to display candles, or hang a candle chandelier in the bathroom and drape with strands of jeweled beads.

Many bathrooms lack good storage space. Place a narrow bookcase in your bathroom or install shelving wherever you can find the space. Paint shelving white or another light color to create the illusion of a larger space. Place bundles of fluffy towels in baskets on your shelves and display pretty soaps and candles. You might even nestle a few favorite books or magazines between interesting bookends for bathroom reading.

Add jeweled color by filling a crystal wine decanter with green or red mouthwash or by displaying a collection of perfume bottles on a silver or mirrored tray. And for greenery and detail, suspend a few green plants or an antique birdcage from the ceiling.

To add texture and lightness to your bathroom, add or change some fabrics. Replace an old shower curtain with one that you really love. Or make your own tab-top curtains from a favorite fabric. Add a light, airy, and romantic ambience with attractive window curtains, made from lacy material. Go ahead and splurge on a cozy bathmat set, and don't forget to hang a couple of thirsty terry robes on the back of the bathroom door.

To add some more inviting touches, consider these possibilities:

❧ Paint the wood frames of pretty prints in a color that matches or accents the bathroom color scheme. Choose prints that make you feel happy or relaxed.

❧ Replace your plain or boring mirror with an intriguing bureau mirror.

❧ Spruce up dull bathroom cabinets by giving them a coat of decorative paint and replacing old pull knobs or handles with gold-tone or crystal ones.

❧ Decorate your bathroom tiles, and even the sink, by painting designs on them with special paints.

❧ Don't underestimate the effect of a new wall color or treatment. Hang fresh wallpaper or paint the walls. Or, to add a great deal of charm, consider a readymade decorative mural that you can easily affix to the wall.

❧ Consider setting up a tea service in your bathroom. I have a large counter in my bathroom where I keep an electric tea maker and a pretty tin of my favorite teas. A cup of herbal tea while bathing is very relaxing.

For Your Bedroom

A romantic setting means something different to each of us. Some may find romance in glowing candles, and others may find it in antique linens or fresh flowers. Whatever your fancy, fill your room with things that are pleasant to you. The bedroom is a place to escape, to rest, and to dream. Enjoy it. Finding just the right sumptuous fabrics for your plush comforters and plump pillows is a great start for designing your dream bedroom. Don't be afraid to mix colors, textures, and patterns as long as you tie them together with a common theme or color. You don't have to go out and buy all new furnishings, either. Mix together antiques and new pieces to create a dramatic style.

Adding romantic touches to your bedroom doesn't have to cost a small fortune. Here are some ideas to consider when decorating your room.

Special Touches

❁ Place a vase of fresh flowers and an elegant candle lamp on your bedside table.

❁ Replace regular light bulbs with pink ones to soften and warm your room. Or add a candle or wall sconce above your bed for mood lighting.

＊ Keep a blank journal book in your bedside drawer to jot down the day's events, note great ideas, or record dreams.

＊ Hang plump tassels on drawer pulls and top a dresser with a tasseled table runner or a small, crocheted tablecloth.

＊ Add instant glamour to a dresser top with a tray of perfume bottles.

＊ Display favorite photos on your walls and shelves to brighten and personalize your room.

＊ Weave fresh greenery such as evergreen, holly, and pine into garlands and hang over doorways and headboards to add a touch of freshness and fragrance. Or drape a garland of silk flowers over your dresser mirror.

＊ Tie some chandelier crystals on transparent fishing line and hang them in front of your window to add sparkle to your room.

＊ Don't forget about wallpaper and paint. Your wall treatment can tie the whole room together and make it work.

Gift Wrapping & Other Creative Ideas

Clever Containers for Candles

❧ Make beautiful container candles utilizing ordinary metal or thick glass containers such as coffee cans, tins, or jam jars. Just fill with soft wax and insert a wick with a metal base clip while wax is still liquefied, and voila! You've got a great candle with a touch of country charm.

❧ Create a beautiful accent candle by filling English pottery (small blue and white bowls) with soft wax and inserting a wick while hot. These pretty little containers make stunning container candles and add charm and light to any room in your home.

❧ Make a nice candle for the garden by filling a terra cotta pot or ceramic container with soft wax. Seal the hole with mold sealing wax and fill with melted soft wax. Insert a wick with a metal base clip into hot wax. With a hot glue gun, decorate the outside of the container with pretty dried flowers.

Creative Wrapping and Presentation for Candles

Wrapping and packaging your homemade creations makes these delightful formulas and projects even more appealing when you're giving them as gifts. Here are some ways to make good gifts great gifts.

✿ Wrap finished candles in clear cellophane bags and secure with a pretty ribbon for a nice, finished look. You can wrap these fabulous candles in pretty gift baskets and nestle them in grass, tissue paper, or even potpourri. (You can also add a few scent-coordinated soaps for a great gift!)

✿ Add a special touch by wrapping a band of homemade paper around the outside of a pillar candle or by tying a pretty ribbon around your candle. Add a few dried flowers or a sprig of dried herbs to the bow for a natural look.

✿ Stencil pretty designs onto candles with paint, or paint designs or pictures onto candles using acrylic craft paints.

Special Ideas for Soaps

✿ Make miniature guest soaps by molding soap in candy molds.

✿ Make a loaf of soap by increasing your ingredients to fill a loaf pan.

✿ Coat the back of a dried leaf or dried flower with white glue to decorate a plain bar of soap.

✿ Glue on decoupage cut-outs to dress up a bar of soap.

✿ Add designs to your soap by rubberstamping directly on the soap bar. (Gold ink is particularly nice for this.)

✿ Use an empty one-quart milk carton as a mold to make about a pound of soap. Give the loaf as a gift along with a cheese cutter, and include instructions to slice off bars as they're needed. (Similar 1-pound soap loaves sell for more than $30!)

Creative Wrapping and Presentation for Soaps

As if homemade soaps weren't nice enough, you can create some really fabulous looks with creative wrapping. Here are a few ideas:

❦ Bundle your soaps in pretty tissue paper or unusual wrapping paper and tape them up like miniature presents.

❦ Tie your soap with strands of natural raffia or use sheer, sparkly ribbons for a natural, earthy look.

❦ Use waxed paper and tissue paper on bars of soap for a great presentation.

❦ Make your own soap boxes out of thick card stock paper. Open up a regular soap box and lay it down flat. Then trace its shape onto your card stock. Cut it out with scissors, making sure to include all slits. Then duplicate the box folds, insert your soap and glue, then close.

❦ Make another fun soap package from corrugated cardboard. Form a piece into a small tube that will fit your bar of soap. Wrap the soap in tissue paper and insert it inside the box.

❦ Make picture perfect soaps! Wrap a bar in bridal illusion or other sheer fabric and tie it at the top with a pretty ribbon. (Soap wrapped this way can be used as a drawer sachet too!)

Marketplace

You CAN locate many of the ingredients needed for these projects in craft stores, through Internet suppliers, health stores, or your local drugstore. Some of the specialty ingredients may be more difficult to obtain, especially if you live in a small town. However, the following recommended suppliers can provide everything you will need for these crafts by mail order.

Soap and Toiletry-Making Supplies

General Bottle Supply
1930 E. 51st St.
Los Angeles, California 90058
(800) 782-0198
Offers a wide selection of glass, plastic, and perfume bottles. Call or write for a free catalog.

Lorann Oils
P.O. Box 22009
4518 Aurelius Rd.
Lansing, Michigan 48909-2009
(800) 248-1302
Offers a wide variety of flavor oils, candy-making supplies, and essential oils.

San Francisco Herb Company
250 14th St.
San Francisco, California 94103
(800) 227-4530
You can get your dried herbs, dried flowers, or potpourri ingredients here.

Sunburst Bottle Company
5710 Auburn Blvd., Suite #7
Sacramento, California 95841
(916) 348-5576
Here you'll find a wide selection of glass, plastic, and perfume bottles. Send $2 for their catalog.

Valley Hills Press
3400 Earles Fork Rd.
Sturgis, Mississippi 39769
(800) 323-7102
You can order books about traditional soapmaking through this company.

Victorian Essence
P.O. Box 1220
Arcadia, California 91077
(888) 446-5455
Web site: www.Victorian-Essence.com
This supplier offers a complete line of toiletry-making supplies, including perfume oils, essential oils, cosmetic oils, unscented soaps, soap molds, foaming concentrate, glycerin, aloe vera gel, mica dust, cosmetic clays, bottles, containers, labels, and kits for beginners. Call or write for a free catalog or visit their Web site.

Candlemaking Supplies

General Wax and Candle Company
P.O. Box 9398
North Hollywood, California 91609
(800) WAX-STOR
Web site: www.genwax.com
Provides access to a full line of candlemaking supplies, including molds, wax, additives, books, colors, fragrances, and beginner kits. Call or write for a free catalog.

INDEX

Oils, Lotions & Other Luxuries

Kelly Reno

A handmade gift is the ultimate expression of friendship and love—especially when that gift is something soothing and luxurious. This inspiring book offers easy recipes for silky lotions, extravagant oils, and fragrant skin care products you can make at home. Includes recipes for Super Light Honeydew Moisturizer, Five-Oil Massage Blend, Rose Bath Beads, Tingling Mint Toner, and many more luxurious indulgences.

ISBN 0-7615-2544-0 / Hardcover
96 pages / U.S. $14.95 / Can. $22.95

(800) 632-8676, ext. 4444 · www.primalifestyles.com

Perfumes, Scented Gifts & Other Fragrances

Kelly Reno

Create wonderfully unique fragrances—to keep or give away. Based on fresh, natural ingredients, Kelly Reno fashions personalized scents for both women and men. Women's fragrances include such recipes as Spirited, Masquerade, and Bright Eyes. Men's colognes include Northern Lights, Adventure, and Outdoorsman. Includes simple yet elegant ideas for bottling, boxing, and wrapping these luxuries.

ISBN 0-7615-2341-3 / Hardcover
96 pages / U.S. $14.95 / Can. $22.95

(800) 632-8676, ext. 4444 · www.primalifestyles.com

Soaps, Shampoos & Other Suds

Kelly Reno

*I*magine the most simple ingredients—herbs, flowers, and pure soaps. Kelly Reno shows you how to work magic with these natural basics and turn them into indulgent treasures. These are simple, yet divine recipes made from the freshest ingredients. Includes recipes for Coffee and Cream Soap, Georgia Peach Shower Gel, and Peppermint Clarifying Shampoo.

ISBN 0-7615-2543-2 / Hardcover
96 pages / U.S. $14.95 / Can. $22.95

(800) 632-8676, ext. 4444 · www.primalifestyles.com

To Order Books

I'd like to order copies of the following titles:

Quantity	Title	Amount
_____	*Oils, Lotions & Other Luxuries*	_____
_____	*Perfumes, Scented Gifts & Other Fragrances*	_____
_____	*Soaps, Shampoos & Other Suds*	_____
	Subtotal	_____
	7.25% Sales Tax (CA only)	_____
	7% Sales Tax (PA only)	_____
	5% Sales Tax (IN only)	_____
	7% G.S.T. Tax (Canada only)	_____
	Priority Shipping	_____
	Total Order	_____

FREE
Ground Freight
in U.S. and Canada

Foreign and priority shipping requests call
(916) 787-7000
for price quote

By Telephone: With American Express, MC, or Visa, call 800-632-8676 ext. 4444, Monday–Friday, 8:30–4:30.

www.primapublishing.com

By E-mail: sales@primapub.com

By Mail: Just fill out the information below and send with your remittance to:
Prima Publishing · P.O. Box 1260BK · Rocklin, CA 95677

Name _____

Address _____

City _____ State _____ ZIP _____

MC/Visa/American Express# _____ Exp. _____

Check/money order enclosed for $ _____ Payable to Prima Publishing

Daytime telephone _____

Signature _____